<u>**Instructor's Manual**</u>

to

Accompany

<u>MAKING PEACE</u>

A Reading/Writing/Thinking Text
on Global Community

Elaine Brooks
Brooklyn College, City University of New York

Len Fox
Brooklyn College, City University of New York

St. Martin's Press   New York

CAMBRIDGE
UNIVERSITY PRESS

32 Avenue of the Americas, New York NY 10013-2473, USA

Cambridge University Press is part of the University of Cambridge.

It furthers the University's mission by disseminating knowledge in the pursuit of education, learning and research at the highest international levels of excellence.

www.cambridge.org
Information on this title: www.cambridge.org/9780521657792

Copyright © 1995 by St. Martin's Press, Inc.
© Cambridge University Press 2014

First published 1995

A catalogue record for this publication is available from the British Library

ISBN 978-0-521-65779-2 Paperback

CONTENTS

Part IV: Cross-Cultural Encounters

Part V: Spiritual Values

Part VI: Working for a Better World

INTRODUCTION

The authors have written <u>Making Peace: A Reading/Writing/ Thinking Text on Global Community</u> with two goals in mind. One is to help students (high intermediate/advanced ESL, as well as basic reading/writing) to develop their language skills. We will comment subsequently on how the various types of exercises can help to achieve this goal. The second goal is to give students a chance to read/think/discuss/write with their classmates about themes related to peace education. The authors have in recent years been developing and teaching thematic units and courses on such topics as the environment, multiculturalism, community, and creating a more peaceful world. In teaching such courses, we do not only want students to think about the topics, but also to focus in their thinking not just on their individual lives but on the lives of others in their immediate environment, in their country, and in other countries throughout the world. We hope that students will acquire the belief that the world can become a more peaceful place and the desire to work toward that goal. In other words, we aim to develop not only language and thinking ability, but also better values and character in our students. We assume that the teachers who have chosen to use this book have similar goals for their students, and are grateful that you have joined us in this challenging mission.

We have divided the text into six sections, which are all connected to the broadly defined topic of peace education ("creating a more peaceful world"). Section I raises consciousness about the need to act in a more responsible way in relation to our environment. Section II examines sources of conflict related to men's and women's roles, and ways of resolving these conflicts. If we wish to have a more peaceful world in the future, we must raise children who will desire this goal, and who will acquire the skills and attitudes needed to achieve it (the topic of Section III). Section IV raises the point that a peaceful world will depend on our ability to get along with people of diverse backgrounds; our present lack of such ability is a tragic source of violence and war in the world today. One possible source of inspiration, discussed in Section V, is religion or spirituality, which, at its best, teaches us to be aware and concerned about something bigger than our individual self. Section VI presents the ideas of a number of individuals who have been effective teachers and workers for world peace (including two recent winners of the Nobel Peace Prize).

THE EXERCISES

We have already made some comments on the exercises in the preface to the student text, but will make further comments below.

Getting Ready to Read

Reading is not just a matter of looking at words and receiving meaning. An important aspect of reading is motivation. If students are interested in a topic that they are about to read about, if the topic seems important to them, they are likely to focus, to concentrate, to think as they read, to read critically -- to try hard to understand and to get something out of their reading. The goal of discussing words in the title and from a text, and of discussing questions on the general topic (or doing a prewriting activity in place of this) is to arouse the interest of the students and to elicit their background knowledge. In discussing the title, a teacher can ask students to define one or two words in the title, then comment on how these concepts are related to the following reading. One way to do the key vocabulary is to ask students if they don't understand some of the words/concepts and to ask other students to define those word/concepts. Students can think and write something for five minutes about the pre-reading questions, then discuss what they have written with a classmate or with the whole class. The teacher should write responses to the pre-reading questions (or do a prewriting activity) at the same time as the students do this. This allows her to share her responses with the students and to understand the task that students have been asked to do. After doing all this, students should be well motivated and prepared to read the following text with good comprehension and interest.

Thinking about the Reading

It is the goal of the exercises in this section to ensure that students have literally

1

comprehended the text. The True/False and Comprehension Questions check their comprehension of particular key sentences. The Outline focuses on the overall major ideas and prepares them to write a summary. Probably the best way to check overall comprehension of a text is to have students write a summary. In fact, for advanced students, the teacher may simply require that they write a summary. If they are able to do this without doing the preliminary exercises, that is fine. The goal of the preliminary exercises is to help students who are having some difficulty with language and/or reading/writing skills -- to give them practice, support, and guidance so that they will be prepared to write a good summary.

The authors have noticed that students tend to copy answers from a text. This does not allow them to use their own language, and, in fact, does not clearly indicate that they understand a question or even their own answer. We have therefore stressed in this book that direct copying from a text is unacceptable. Over the semester, the teacher can write examples of bad and good answers that students have written, or actually develop answers with students on a blackboard in order to teach them the skill of paraphrasing as opposed to direct copying.

Making Connections

Literal comprehension of reading is not an adequate goal for students, expecially for texts such as those in this book, which are intended to encourage students to think so deeply that their values and character can be affected. Such deep thinking involves going beyond the text in order to reflect on one's own experiences, and going to other sources in order to learn more about a topic of interest. The varied activities suggested in this section include writing about one's experiences, finding and writing about a picture, finding and writing about a related passage, and interviewing someone. These activities would be particularly useful to intermediate ESL students who need to develop fluency and listening/speaking ability. If the teacher has advanced students who wish to focus on writing essays and has limited class time, he may wish to skip most of these activities. It is essential however that the students be expected to react critically to the reading and that some time in class be devoted to discussing their critical reaction. A major reason for this is that if students know this is going to happen, they will do the reading much more carefully in the first place.

Getting Ready to Write

We have commented extensively on the prewriting activities in the preface to the student text. Perhaps the most important point to stress is that the goal of the writing is for students to find a topic that they are truly interested in, to think deeply about this topic, and to produce a piece of writing that is not only well organized, well developed, and grammatically correct, but which allows them to relate their own experience and creative thought to a topic that they care about. In this way, discussion and writing can become part of a significant learning experience. Toward that goal, the authors have tried to select thought-provoking texts on important topics, to provide interesting activities and questions for students to choose from. The teacher must get involved in the topics under discussion, share her own thoughts, make it clear that she cares about the topics, make thought-provoking comments before prewriting and discussion activities -- make every effort to get students engaged in thinking, communicating, and learning.

One way to do the "Planning an Essay" exercise is for the teacher to choose one student and to help this student to develop an outline on the board while the rest of the class is watching and listening (having a "fishbowl conference" with the student). The teacher could help the student to develop a clear thesis that the student really wants to write about, and to think of specific examples that can be used in the writing, being sure not to just write vague, boring general statements with no support.

Revising/Editing Your Writing

It is important to stress that students who are having trouble with writing will not be able to correctly evaluate their essay according to the questions on the "Revising Checklist." They will not know if they have presented a clear thesis, included only relevant information, given good examples and details. Over the semester, the teacher must present good models, have conferences with

2

students, let students have conferences among themselves in pairs or groups. As the semester progresses, students should begin to understand the questions on the checklist and become better able to evaluate their essays according to these criteria.

It is probably even more difficult for students to evaluate their essay according to the questions on the "Editing Checklist." (Is there correct punctuation, use of articles, use of verbs, use of word forms, etc.?) Students tell the authors that if they knew the correct grammar, they wouldn't make mistakes, or if they knew how to find and correct their errors themselves, they would do it. So how can we teach them to do this?

For one thing, the authors feel that teachers must not put too early and too heavy an emphasis on correct grammar. It is not advisable when a student is trying to express an important idea to correct the student's grammar. This indicates that you are not so interested in the student's ideas as in her correct use of language. It will make students less willing to express their ideas in the future. Remember the goal of encouraging students to think and communicate freely about the topics under consideration. It also may be advisable to focus on ideas in an early draft of an essay.

At some point however teachers must help students to focus on grammar. Teachers may sometimes explain a grammar point to a class if most of the students do not understand it, or to a group of students, or to individual students in conferences. Often, students understand a grammatical concept but they continue to make "careless mistakes" in their writing. The authors have found it helpful to underline errors, indicate in the margin the type of error, and ask students to correct the error themselves. It is sometimes better not to correct every error so that students can focus on the most serious "patterns of error." Students can be asked to identify and underline particular grammatical units before they hand in their essays (e.g., subjects and verbs, articles and nouns, punctuation) as a way of learning to proofread and edit their writing. Class time can be used for editing, during which students can work together in pairs or groups. Teachers can ask students to focus on one paragraph and try to check for particular types of errors. Hopefully, as the semester progresses, students will become aware of their individual grammatical problems and become better able to correct them.

Research Assignments and Suggested Further Reading

As previously mentioned, this text is aimed at either high intermediate or advanced students. High intermediate students who are interested in developing fluency may spend more time on the activities under "Making Connections," in particular doing interviews if they are concerned about developing oral fluency. Advanced students who are primarily interested in writing and academic skills may choose one of the topics at the end of a section and do a research assignment or paper on it. The teacher should decide which activities are most appropriate for her particular class.

USING THE TEXT

Introducing the Text

It would be appropriate to mention at the beginning of the semester that the goal of the text is to make students aware of aspects of peace education and to encourage them to be concerned about these topics. It would be a good idea to say a few words about some of the authors of the texts and what they have done in their lives. It would be interesting to ask if students can name other individuals who are similar to the text authors in what they have done or how they have lived. By the way, it is also important to make it clear to students that they should feel free to express their honest opinions about any of the topics discussed. If for example they feel sure that war is and will always be necessary, or that world peace is not a possible or even a desirable goal, they must be allowed to express these opinions, as long as they do a good job of supporting them. This sort of freedom is necessary in a writing class in which students must learn to effectively express their own opinions, not those that someone else is trying to impose on them. Of course, if students become somewhat more concerned or optimistic about the possibilities for world peace as a result of this course, that certainly

3

would be, in the opinion of the authors, a positive result.

Over a Few Days

At Brooklyn College, students have two 1 1/2 hour classes per week. The following plan is intended to fit into that schedule, but can be reorganized according to the number and length of classes in a particular program.

Day 1 (first day of the semester)

introductory comments
class discussion of a topic
small group discussions
in class writing

Day 2

read student writing
 revise and edit
pre-reading activities
 discuss title, vocabulary,
 pre-reading questions

Day 3

discuss reading text 1
post reading activities
 T/F Qs, Compr. Qs, Reaction
pre-writing activities
 Freewriting, Disc. & Comp. Qs, Outline

Day 4

read student writing
 revise and edit
pre-reading activities
 ... etc.

Over a Semester

The following plan suggests covering only 4 sections in this book over a 15 week semester by doing one text each week and all four texts in the unit. Another approach would be to do all 6 units but to do only 2 or 3 texts in each one. Teachers and students are free to choose exactly which units and how many texts in each unit they prefer to do (although the authors would recommend doing at least two texts in a unit to establish a thematic unit rather than doing isolated texts which do not seem clearly related to each other).

A 15-week Syllabus:

week 1: introductory
    State of the World, text 1
     one day: working on a piece of writing,
        doing pre-reading activities

4

next day: discussing the assigned rdg.
               beginning a first draft of a
               piece of writing

2: State of the World, text 2
3,4: State of the World, texts 3,4
5-8: Men and Women, texts 1-4
9-12: Spiritual Values, texts 1-4
13-15: Working for A Better World, texts 1,2,4

THE TEXTS

Part I: State of the World

1. The Illusion of Progress
If students are to become concerned about improving the world, they must first of all realize that there are some problems about its current state. This text, from a highly respected, scientifically accurate source, is intended to help them to realize this.

T/F Questions (Paragraphs where the answer is found are indicated) 1. F (3); 2. F (9); 3. T (11); 4. F (12); 5. T (18)

Comprehension Questions Possible answers might be
1. Environmental damage has led to hotter summers, dead lakes, and dying forests. (par. 4)
2. Much cropland has become useless, over-use has changed some grasslands to desert, and the rate of loss of forestland has increased a great deal. (14)
3. GNP measures the value of goods produced and subtracts loss in value of equipment. It does not however count the loss of natural resources. (17)
4. In evaluating a country's economy, we should consider not only loss of natural resources but also negative effects of economic activity on the environment. (20)

Completed Outline

paragraphs
1-2:   Global economic progress since World War II
3-4:   A sense of illusion
5-8:   Negative affects of environment on economy
9-10: Problems in Africa and Latin America
11-13: 3 sources: croplands, forests, grasslands
14-16: Since 1981, less land available
17-18: GNP doesn't count loss of natural
       resources
19-21: Repetto's new system of accounting

2. Land Hunger in Asia
This text personalizes the global crisis more than the last one by discussing individual cases such as those of Abdurrashid Ali Khan and Hassan Ali. While going through the language activities, students should be encouraged to discuss particular cases of poverty that they may know about through their personal experience or reading.

T/F Questions (Paragraphs where the answer is found are indicated) 1. T (1); 2. F (2); 3. T (8); 4. F (12); 5. F (13)

Comprehension Questions Possible answers might be
1. Peasants have less land than their grandfathers because land is divided among children. As people have become poorer, they have been forced to mortgage and sell their land. (par. 5)
2. The land owned by most peasants does not produce enough food to live on. Peasants must also buy fuel and clothing. Even with getting an extra job, peasants don't have enough money to live on. So they are forced to sell their land, and they become still poorer. (7)
3. Wealthy landowners, since 1947, have illegally seized land, sold goods to poor landowners at high prices, given loans at high interest rates, and bought land cheaply. (10-11)
4. A landlord loaned money to Hassan Ali but refused to take the money when Hassan wanted to pay back his mortgage. Hassan spent money on going to court, but the lanlord bribed the court and kept

6

Hassan's land. (14-15)

Completed Outline

paragraphs
1: Increasing poverty in Asia
2: The situation in Bangladesh
3: Land hunger
4: Problems from violent rivers
5: Causes of land shortage
6: Example of Abdurrashid Ali Khan
7: The economics of poverty
8: Natural disasters, 1970-76
9: The situation of middle-income peasants
10: The situation of rich peasants
11: How the rich exploit the poor
12: Example of "tubewells"
13-15: Examples of the unfair legal system

3. Eradicate Nuclear Weapons from the Face of the Earth
Helen Caldicott depicts the appalling conditions in the world and the resulting threats to our survival ("We're on a terminally ill planet") in order to shock people into doing something about it.

T/F Questions (Paragraphs where the answer is found are indicated) 1. T (2); 2. F (4); 3. F (5); 4. F (6); 5. T (8)

Comprehension Questions Possible answers might be
1. The world needs enough food for everyone, medical supplies and care, birth control programs, protection of forests and seas, fair sharing of resources, education, and anti-poverty programs. (par. 5)
2. Caldicott saw a great deal of disease and illiteracy in Cuba before the revolution. She feels that conditions improved after the revolution. (7)
3. After the revolution, she saw a better healthcare system and improved education, but still not many goods in the shops. (7)
4. At the Lucas Aerospace Industry, the workers had a meeting to consider what they could produce rather than military supplies. They took their plans to the management, who agreed to shift to non-military production. (9)

Completed Outline

paragraphs
1: Effects of the atomic bomb
2: Women's feelings about saving babies
3: An ill planet
4: Peace conversion
5: The world's needs
6: Pollution
7: Progress in Cuba
8: Developing a global economic system
9: Example of Lucas Aerospace
10: The responsibility of saving the future

4. Picturing a Sustainable Society
Discussing the idea of "a sustainable society" is one way to force people who are living in a wasteful, irresponsible way to realize that we simply cannot continue to live in this way for long without suffering serious negative consequences.

T/F Questions (Paragraphs where the answer is found are indicated.) 1. F (3); 2. T (4); 3. F (9); 4. T (11); 5. F (16)

Comprehension Questions Possible answers might be
1. Although the World Bank is concerned about the environmental effects of its projects, its member countries do not have an overall plan for achieving sustainability. (par. 6)
2. Nuclear plants are dangerous, produce nuclear wastes, and make it likely that more countries will develop nuclear weapons. (10-11)
3. If the world doesn't develop a more equitable economy, the poorer nations will not be able to afford to create sustainable economies. (15)
4. More important than acquiring material possessions are human relationships, stronger communities, music and the arts. (19-21)

Completed Outline

paragraphs
1-2:   Need a new vision of the future
3:      A sustainable society
4:      Present societies are not sustainable
5:     What not to do
6:     Need an overall plan
7-9:   Three basic ideas
10-11: Solar or nuclear energy?
12-14: Population control
15:     An equitable world economy
16:    Individual values
17-18: Need to change values
19-20: Materialism
21-23: A better future

Part II: Men and Women

5. Where I Come From Is Like This
One of the basic relationships in human life is that between men and women. In this section, students will consider roles men and women play in different cultures, the ways they relate to each other, and how those roles and relations affect the world we live in. This first article provides a step toward examining the factors mentioned above by offering Allen's view of women in her own Native American culture and contrasting it with a view of women in mainstream American culture.

T/F Questions (Paragraphs where the answer is found are indicated.) 1. T (2); 2. T (3); 3. F (4); 4. F (9); 5. T (11)

Comprehension Questions Possible answers might be
1. A primary difference in the ways women are perceived in tribal cultures in contrast to non–Indian cultures is that their identity is strongly connected to their tribe/people. (par. 2)

2. Allen first found negative images of Indian women from non—Indian sources, and these images were more often of Indian men or Indians in general. (5)

3. Allen's understanding of what it meant to be a woman developed through the women she knew, such as her mother and grandmother, and the stories she heard from her mother. (5,8)

4. Occasionally, when trying to gain attention from non—Indians, Allen finds she forgets her "tribal woman's good sense." (13)

Completed Outline

paragraphs

1:   Need to integrate two traditions
2:   Diversity of roles in tribal culture
3:   Limitations of western women's roles
4:   Power of femininity
5–7: Images of tribal women
8:   Learning to be a woman through stories
9–10: Discovery of contradictory views throug formal education
11: Balance of male and female in ritual
12: Learning to be strong and balanced
13: Source of doubts about herself

6. Liza and Family

This text illustrates the daily life of a single, working mother in the former Soviet Union – some of the issues she faces and her feelings about them. Students should be encouraged to share what they perceive of the responsibilities of parents, both men and women, in their own cultures and compare them to Liza's life. In addition, discussion should include ways our society could improve and support family life, thereby relieving the stress and problems that families face.

T/F Questions (Paragraphs where the answer is found are indicated.) 1. T (2,6); 2. F (14) ; 3. T (24); 4. F (36,37); 5. F (37,39)

Comprehension Questions Possible answers might be

1. Both Liza and Emil seem to find separating on Mondays difficult, but Emil adjusts to being with his friends and finds it hard to leave them on Friday. (par.10, 12)

2. Emil's father was upset that Liza didn't give Emil his surname; also, he'd been drafted when Emil was little, so they grew apart. (14)

3. Liza believes she is a bad mother because she rushes around and leaves Emil to amuse himself when she's tired. She also feels she hasn't taught him to have spiritual and ethical values. (31)

4. Abortion is common in the Soviet Union because the contraceptives aren't very good, nor are they easy to get. (36)

Completed Outline

paragraphs

1–3:   Introduction to Liza's life
4–8:   Liza's morning routine
9–12: Emil's weekly boarding school
13–14: Emil's father
15–16: Liza's limited free time
17–24: Importance of having children
25–26: Definition of a good mother
27–29: Definition of a good father

7. American Men Don't Cry

Montagu discusses how American men are influenced by the expectation that they should not cry and how boys are conditioned not to cry. He asks us to consider the effect of depriving human beings of this natural activity. Class discussion might cover the expectations various cultures have for men and women and the consequences of those expectations — on individuals, on relations between men and women, and on our society as a whole.

T/F Questions (Paragraphs where the answer is found are indicated.) 1. F (1); 2. T (1); 3. F (2); 4. T (3); 5. T (4)

Comprehension Questions Possible answers might be

1. Women and children are allowed to cry in certain circumstances. (par. 1)
2. Boys are discouraged from crying whenever they feel like it by being called "sissies" or "cry–babies" if they do. (2)
3. Being unable to cry is bad because it deprives the human being of his ability to restore his emotional balance. (3)
4. Being unable to cry is unhealthy and makes one less human. (4)

Completed Outline

paragraphs
1: Why American men don't cry
2: How they are trained not to cry
2–3: Why it is bad not to cry
4: Inability to cry makes one less human

8. Machismo in Washington

Stone's article also considers the connections between expectations for male behavior and the larger society, but it takes readers beyond the individual and asks us to examine how sex role stereotypes may influence politics and the relations between nations, including our chances for world peace. Students might hypothesize how/if the world would differ if more women were active in governmental and diplomatic positions.

T/F Questions (Paragraphs where the answer is found are indicated.) 1. T (1); 2. F (3,4); 3. F (5); 4. T (7); 5. T (15)

Comprehension QuestionsPossible answers might be

1. Some of the reasons given for the bombing of Vietnam were the need to stand up to the aggressor, to prove national will, and to prevent the President from appearing intimidated. (par. 2)
2. In the nuclear age, a particular problem with small boy statecraft is the possibility of a worldwide catastrophe. (7)
3. Stone believes that politicians alone are not responsible for such machismo, but they act in this way because a number of people within any nation also see war as a test of will. (7)
4. Small boy statesmanship is problematic even when it appears to "succeed" because of the cost

10

involved, the number of people who suffer and die as a consequence of it. (16)

Completed Outline

paragraphs
1:   Comparison of the Seven Immortals to supporters of bombing of Vietnam
2–3:   Machismo politics of US to Vietnam
4–5:   Small boy tactics applied to war
6:   To avoid appearing "chicken"
7:   Individual political risks outweigh danger to the world
8:   Circumstances among superpowers
9:   Whose turf and whose laws?
10:   Superpowers do not consult allies
11:   Effect of Nixon's strategy
12–14: Danger of reacting too quickly
15:   Potential for destruction of the world
16:   Cost of macho politics

Part III: Children, Family, and Education

9. Grandparents Have Copped Out

Mead's article focuses on the extended family, specifically the role that grandparents play and the function they served in society in the past. Class discussion may cover both how grandparents fit into a variety of cultures and Mead's belief that the way people age needs to change.

T/F Questions (Paragraphs where the answer is found are indicated) 1. F (1); 2. T (3); 3. F (5); 4. T (8,9); 5. T (12)

Comprehension Questions Possible answers might be
1. The main thing older Americans do at present for the younger generation is to not bother them by seeing them too often or complaining. (par. 4)
2. This emphasis has isolated young and old from each other so that young people lack perspective on life which they could get from their elders. (5)
3. According to Mead, menopause is a means of allowing women to live longer which enables them to share their knowledge with younger people. (7)
4. Mead believes that the function of old people has changed, that old people today have seen many changes and can contribute their knowledge about change to the young to help them understand the past and present as well as plan the future. (8)

Completed Outline

paragraphs
1:   Need for a new style of aging
2:   Ideal of independence and autonomy
3:   Family units
4:   "Not being a burden"
5–6:   Generational perspective
7:   What the old contributed
8–9:   What the old can contribute
10–13: Ways the old have changed
14–15: Finding "a new style of aging"

11

10. From Affirming Diversity

Hoang Vinh's own words can help readers begin a cross–cultural discussion about education and family. One step toward increasing world peace is better understanding and acceptance of cultural perspectives that differ from our own. Students may also consider ways that they, similar to Hoang Vinh, maintain values they grew up with while also taking in new perspectives.

T/F Questions (Paragraphs where the answer is found are indicated) 1. F (1,2); 2. T (6); 3. T (11); 4. F (16–21); 5. T (27)

Comprehension Questions Possible answers might be
1. Vinh feels it is helpful when teachers spend time with students and tell them what to study and how to study. (par. 9)
2. Vinh would like to marry a Vietnamese girl so his children will learn Vietnamese. (14)
3. Vinh became "mental" when he came to the United States and was homesick; he couldn't eat, sleep or enjoy himself because he was sad. (16–21)
4. Vinh values his language and culture and admires his people. He hopes to share these values with his children. (22–24)

Completed Outline

paragraphs
1:     Definition of "educated"
2–3:   American and Vietnamese school systems
4–5:   Grades
6:     Purpose of education
7–11: What helps students to learn
12–13: Vinh's goals
14–15: Thoughts about culture and family
16–21: Adjustment problems
22–25: Feelings about Vietnamese culture
26–27: Teachers' understanding of students
28–30: Feelings about use of first language
31–35: Maintaining culture
36–37: Correspondence with parents

11. An Education in Language

The Rodriguez article considers some of the same questions as the preceding text, but comes to different conclusions at times. It also provides students with the chance to think about how language influences their sense of who they are and how they fit into the society they live in. Questions about assimilation and social success may help students to examine more closely the relations among various groups in a multicultural society.

T/F Questions (Paragraphs where the answer is found are indicated) 1. F (1); 2. T (1,2); 3. T (6,7); 4. F (8); 5. F (20)

Comprehension Questions Possible answers might be
1. Rodriguez describes himself as "a socially dis advantaged child" because he didn't realize he had a right to use "public language" and so he felt isolated from society outside of his family. (par. 2)
2. The advantage of his parents' use of English at home was that Rodriguez finally felt able to parti cipate like other children in school; the disadvantage, however, was that he felt angry and deprived of

12

intimacy at home. (6–8)

3. His mother was unable to advance further at work because her employers found her limitations in English unacceptable for more advanced positions. (16)

4. Although they did not keep him from going away to college, Rodriguez's parents were sad that he wished to leave, that he seemed separate from them. (20)

Completed Outline

<u>paragraphs</u>

1–2:   Young Rodriguez's need to learn the "public language"
3:      Classroom language
4–5 : His family's difficulty with English
6:      Effects of his parents' use of English at home
7–8 : Sense of loss at home
9:      Teachers as authorities
10–11: Withdrawal from parents
12–13: Mixed feelings toward parents and school
14:     Importance of education to his parents
15–16: His mother's own ambition
17:     Rodriguez's desire to be a teacher
18–19: Sense of separation from his parents
20:     Rodriguez's departure for college

12. Children and War

People tend to think of adults, specifically men, when they think about warfare. Boothby's article forces readers to recognize the increasing involvement of civilians and especially children in modern warfare. His call for all people to take responsiblity for the rights of children can be a catalyst for getting students to think of ways that we can act, individually and together, to provide children with a peaceful world in which to grow.

T/F Questions (Paragraphs where the answer is found are indicated) 1. F (4); 2. T (8); 3. T (9–11); 4. T (12); 5. F (13)

Comprehension Questions Possible answers might be

1. Children have become increasingly involved in wars because methods of war have changed and there is less distinction between civilians and combatants; in addition, children have become deliberate targets of war as a way of terrorizing their families. (par. 5,8)

2. Children may be forced into participating in war through indoctrination, lack of food and protection, or under physical threat. (9–11)

3. We have legislation to protect children, but Boothby believes we do not have the will or means to use it. (12)

4. A viable organization to protect the basic rights of children might be one way to protect them better in the future, but an organization alone cannot do it. People must be responsible for protecting children's rights. (13–14)

Completed Outline

<u>paragraphs</u>

1–3: Guatemalan child's story as example of modern war
4:     Rise in wartime deaths of civilians
5:     Changing nature of war
6–7:   Children targeted as retaliation

8: Children as pawns in war
9: Indoctrination of child soldiers
10–11: Turning children into soldiers
12: Lack of will/means to implement legislation
13: Inadequate safeguarding of children's rights
14: Necessity for all of us to be responsible

Part IV: Cross–Cultural Encounters

13. The Arab World

The Hall text allows readers to expand on the discussion begun with the comparison in the preceding article by considering new factors such as space and privacy. Similar to I.F. Stone's "Machismo and Washington," Hall's piece helps readers to consider the ways that factors such as sterotypes of male behavior or (mis)perceptions of cultural behavior can affect not only individual relations but also those among nations.

T/F Questions (Paragraphs where the answer is found are indicated) 1. F (1); 2. T (3); 3. F (10–11); 4. T (12); 5. T (14, 16)

Comprehension Questions Possible answers might be
1. Americans tend to assume that when moving through space, such as on public roads, the bigger, faster, heavier, or more powerful vehicle has the right of
way. In contrast, Arabs find the American attitude annoying because they feel imposed upon by someone who moves into their space if they are also moving,
such as when someone cuts them off. (par. 6)
2. Arabs usually find privacy through such nonphysical means as withdrawing or not speaking. (12)
3. The American practice of being polite by not breathing on someone is interpreted by Arabs as being an indication of shame. (14)
4. Because people perceive the world differently, these differences influence their interpersonal relations and approaches to politics.

Completed Outline

paragraphs
1: Proxemic research on Arab/Westerner relations
2: Arabs and Americans consider each other "pushy"
3: American zone of privacy in public places
4: Conflict regarding public space
5: Arab perception of of public space as "public"
6: Manners/rights of the road
7: Arab assumptions about the body in "space"
8: The "person" in relation to the body
9: Arab sense of self is reflected in the language
10: Cultural adaption to population density
11: Arab use of space at home
12: No talking = privacy
13: Distance–setting mechanisms in Arab culture
14: Olfaction prominent in Arab world
15: Arab link between sense of smell and interper sonal relations
16: Olfactory boundary as distance–setting mechanism

14

17: Cultural differences in proxemic patterns create different perceptions of the world

14. **Anglo vs. Chicano: Why?**
Sometimes it is helpful to be able to stand back from the present and look at a situation of conflict in its larger, historical context in order to understand it better. Campa's article illustrates this in regard to Anglo–Chicano relations in the United States. Students may investigate and discuss other cross–cultural conflicts that they are aware of or interested in as well as Campa's belief that such differences need not be irreconciliable.

T/F Questions (Paragraphs where the answer is found are indicated) 1. F (1–2); 2. T (4); 3. T (9); 4. F (16); 5. T (17)

Comprehension Questions Possible answers might be
1. He begins his contrast by discussing historical sources of differences in language and values prior to and after the arrival of the Spanish and the English in the New World. (par. 2)
2. The Spanish culture was equestrian, which meant they used horses to travel far more than to work the land, which affected their perspective differently than the English who mainly used horses for agricultural purposes and so felt close to their land. (5–6)
3. Hispanic peoples consider individualism as resistance to collectivity, which infringes on personal freedom, so they have few if any fixed rules. Anglo–Americans prefer fixed rules and plans, achieving individualism through action and self–determination. The Anglos value "objectivity," while the Hispanos rely on emotions. (7–8)
4. The English sense of time running quickly is based on their emphasis on the future and that time is money; Hispanos focus on the present until it is gone, which makes their sense of time seem slower. (11)

Completed Outline

paragraphs
1: Cultural differences that can cause conflict
2: Differences implicit in language and values due to historical circumstances
3: Absolutist Anglos; relativist Hispanos
4: Different motives for coming
5–6: Horsemen vs. farmers
7: Individualism versus collectivity
8: Fixed rules versus momentary emotion
9: Courtesy
10: Sharing material goods
11–12: Time differences
13–14: Being versus doing
15: Financial matters
16: Same words, different meanings
17: Conflicts can be reconciled

15. **Living in Two Cultures**
Houston's writing illustrates on a personal level how individuals from different cultures work out their differences, coexist, and even benefit from incorporating two cultures within a marriage and family. Students may share their own experiences with "cultural hybridness" and discuss the concerns that

15

arise in such situations and a variety of ways that these concerns may be handled.

T/F Questions (Paragraphs where the answer is found are indicated) 1. T (2); 2. F (6); 3. T (7–9); 4. T (11); 5. T (19)

Comprehension Questions Possible answers might be
1. After her family returned from the camps, she spent a lot of time with Caucasian friends and school activities, taking on values different from those of her parents. (par. 4–5)
2. Her brothers warned her against Caucasian men who they believed would take advantage of her as a Japanese female, not understanding or valuing her. (8–9)
3. Houston explains that among the Japanese, serving another is not resented or considered degrading, as it may be seen by Americans; she felt an important part of her family when performing her duties. (14–15)
4. Houston found her role as wife confusing at times when she didn't know whether to follow her Japanese or American instincts about how to behave or what to expect. (16–18)

Completed Outline

paragraphs
1:      Early memories of being an Asian female
2:      Family duties as a small child
3:      Papa as authority
4–5:   Her world changed
6:      Breaking social barriers
7:      Japanese/Hakujin conflicts
8:      Brothers' warnings about American men
9:      Discomfort of her double identity
10:    Wanted both cultures in a spouse
11:    Mother's acceptance of husband–to–be
12 :   Confusion about role as wife
13:    Mother's effect on her
14:    Cultural differences with regard to serving others
15:    How Japanese attitude helped her
16:    Cultural differences in marriage
17–18: Effects of cultural differences socially
19:    Acceptance of cultural hybridness
20:    Hopes for her biracial children

16. The Ways of Meeting Oppression
King's article offers an arguement for nonviolence as a means of achieving justice and resisting oppression. In one way or another, all of the authors have tried to suggest ways for us to understand and respect each other in order to improve the relations that exist among us. It should be useful for students to consider some of the basic factors, such as fear and hatred, that King includes in his arguement and how these factors still influence different situations that exist all over the world today.

T/F Questions(Paragraphs where the answer is found are indicated) 1. T (1); 2. F (2–3); 3. F (7); 4. F (9); 5. T (9)

Comprehension Questions Possible answers might be
1. King believes acquiescence is unacceptable because it is not only cowardly but a form of cooperation with evil; thus it is immoral. (par. 3)
2. Although violence appears to be successful at times, its results are temporary because it doesn't

solve problems; it is destructive and immoral. (4–5)

3. Nonviolent resistance tries to reconcile the need to avoid physical aggression while still resisting evil. (7)

4. King seems to suggest that nonviolent resistance can appeal to many because it resists injustice, not specific people but a specific condition. (10)

Completed Outline

paragraphs

1: Why the oppressed may choose acquiescence
2: Some give up
3: To acquiesce is immoral
4: Violence may bring temporary victory
5: Violence is impractical and immoral
6: Bitterness & chaos as results of violence
7: Nonviolent resistance tries to reconcile opposites
8: Nonviolent resistance is useful for racial crisis
9: Benefits of nonviolent resistance
10: Nonviolent resistance enlists consciences

Part V: Spiritual Values

17. From Who Needs God

Discussing the Holocaust, as Kushner does at the beginning of this text, is a good way to arouse people's conscience about the horrors of war and the need to work for a world in which such things will never happen again.

T/F Questions (Paragraphs where the answer is found are indicated.) 1. F (2-5); 2. T (9); 3. F (13); 4. T (15); 5. F (18-24)

Comprehension Questions Possible answers might be

1. Hitler was wrong because our human conscience tells us that he was wrong. (pars. 2-7)

2. In a religious system of many gods, different gods may have different opinions, so it is not clear what is right. (8-9)

3. Morality cannot be determined by vote because certain things, like stealing, are just clearly wrong. There are standards that come from God. (10)

4. "The eyes of the Lord are on your land" means that God makes demands on us and cares about how we live our lives. (20–27)

Completed Outline

paragraphs

1:    teaching about the Holocaust
2-7:   why Hitler was wrong
8-9:   monotheism vs. many gods
10:    moral standards from God
11-12: two possibilities
13-14: the Clint Eastwood movie
15-17: a sense of injustice
18-24: the Unitarian minister's story
25:    story of Kushner's grandfather
26-27: the eyes of God

18. From <u>Freedom from Fear</u>

Aung San Suu Kyi arouses feelings of spirituality by discussing the need "to remain uncorrupted," and by referring to such spiritual leaders as Gandhi and her own father, Aung San. And she herself of course represents that freedom from fear that she wishes to inspire in others.

T/F Questions (Paragraphs where the answer is found are indicated.) 1. T (2); 2. F (3); 3. T (5); 4. T (6); 5. F (11)

Comprehension Questions Possible answers might be

1. Dissatisfaction in Burma has come fron economic hardships, bad government policies, inflation, lower incomes. But more than anything else, it has come from corruption and fear. (par. 3)

2. Aung San told the Burmese people to develop courage, not to depend on others, to be willing to make sacrifices. (3)

3. By "a revolution of the spirit," Aung San Suu Kyi means a change in attitudes such that people become determined to overcome desire, ill will, ignorance and fear, in order to achieve freedom. (6)

4. Gandhi and Aung San were similar in that they taught fearlessness and truth, called for action, and always thought of the good of the masses. (8-9)

Completed Outline

paragraphs

1-2: Fear corrupts

3:   Public dissatisfaction in Burma

4:   Advantages of the rule of law

5:   Relationship between politics and ethics

6:   Revolution of the spirit

7:   The nature of free men

8:   About Aung San (the father)

9:   About Gandhi

10: The nature of courage

11: Causes and effects of fear

12: The source of courage

19. The Simplicity of Love

Krishnamurti uses simple examples from everyday life (tearing at flowers, picking up a stone, not sitting with the villagers at a meeting) to point out people's basic values. Certainly, if we took his advice, we would be following the wise maxim "Think globally, act locally" in an effort to transform the world.

T/F Questions (Paragraphs where the answer is found are indicated.) 1. F (2); 2. T (4); 3. T (6); 4. F (8); 5. F (15)

Comprehension Questions Possible answers might be

1. "Simple love" is being considerate, gentle, sensitive so that you don't want to do harm to people, animals, or flowers. (par. 5)

2. Teachers should have love in their hearts, and should show it in their conversation, in their work, in all their actions. (10)

3. We want to be seen as "important people" because we feel empty. We need others to tell us that we have value. (13-16)

4. The mind does not want to look at its evil actions too closely because it might have to force us to

18

stop doing things that are superficially pleasurable such as smoking. (20-21)

Completed Outline

paragraphs
1-3: Tearing at flowers
4: Removing a stone from the road
5-7: Being sensitive
8-9: Feeling love
10: What a teacher can do
11: The importance of love
12-17: On how "important people" act
18-19: Difference between need and greed
20-21: The mind's evil ways

20. Environmentalism of the Spirit
At the time that the authors are writing this book, Al Gore is vice-president of the United States, and the Clinton administration is developing a much more responsible policy toward the environment than did the Reagan/Bush administrations. It shows that those who have visions of a better world can be not just idealists living in an ivy tower but also realistic individuals with the power to bring about the changes that they envision.

T/F Questions (Paragraphs where the answer is found are indicated.) 1. T (2); 2. F (3); 3. F (5); 4. T (7); 5. T (8)

Comprehension Questions Possible answers might be
1. Sikhism tells us that we can learn patience and love from earth, mobility and liberty from air, warmth and courage from fire, equality and broad-mindedness from sky, purity and cleanliness from water. (par. 4)
2. Perhaps because it developed during the age of industrialism, Baha'i warns that man can have a greatly negative effect on the environment, which will then hurt him. (5)
3. Pope John Paul II calls upon humankind to respect the environment as well as respecting other humans. (6)
4. The Bible warns that environmental destruction will result from going against God's will. (8)

Completed Outline

paragraphs
1: Religions and the earth
2-3: The sacred quality of water
4: Sikh teachings
5: Baha'i teachings
6-7: Teachings of the Pope
8-9: Judeo-Christian teachings
10: Lovelock's theory about the earth
11: A spiritual response
12-13: Seeing God in the world

21. Stages of Community Making

Throughout his book The Different Drum (from which this text is taken), Peck describes the longing for community both in his own life and in the lives of others. Our lifestyle in the modern world pushes us to be isolated, cut off, indifferent, disconnected from others. "Why should I care about others?" many would ask. The best answer is that we are not separate from others, and that it is through caring for others that we can ultimately give our lives meaning.

T/F Questions (Paragraphs where the answer is found are indicated.) 1. F (3–4); 2. F (15); 3. T (17); 4. T (22); 5. F (23)

Comprehension Questions Possible answers might be
1. During the chaos stage, people disagree with each other in an unproductive way. They do not listen to each other. (par. 15)
2. In the community stage, people may disagree, but they listen to each other and succeed in producing positive results. (15)
3. Group members are not interested in emptiness because they do not want to give up their ideas and open their minds to new ones. (19)
4. Peck feels that he should not control a group too much because community can only be produced by the whole group, not by a leader. (26)

Completed Outline

paragraphs
1:      Stages of community
2-5:   About pseudocommunity
6-16:   About chaos
17-20: About emptiness
21-26: Barriers to communication
27-30: About community

22. Understand What Needs to Be Done

Seeing that the original nation-states of the United States had great difficulty among themselves before they agreed to live by the "force of Law" supports the notion that this same thing could be accomplished some day on an international level. As Ferencz points out to skeptics, much in the direction of achieving this goal has already been accomplished.

T/F Questions (Paragraphs where the answer is found are indicated.) 1. T (7); 2. F (8); 3. T (9-11); 4. F (16); 5. F (19)

Comprehension Questions Possible answers might be
1. In the Wild West, anyone with a gun could make and enforce a law. (par. 5)
2. Right after the Revolutionary War, the states were supposed to follow the rules of the "Articles of Confederation" but they didn't. The U.S. wasn't truly a nation at that time. (10-11)
3. The small and large states disagreed on how many representatives each state would have. (15-16)
4. The people of the thirteen states were from different nations, had different customs, different languages, and different religions. (17)

Completed Outline

23. The Need for Solidarity

Aung San Suu Kyi points out that what we can accomplish as individuals is little compared to what we can accomplish as a vast, growing, increasingly well-organized body of people devoted to making peace.

T/F Questions (Paragraphs where the answer is found are indicated.) 1. T (2); 2. F (4); 3. T (7); 4. F (9), 5. T (11)

Comprehension Questions Possible answers might be
1. When people get involved in politics, they may get more political rights. (par. 3)
2. We should not threaten children because it is better to explain to them what is the right thing to do. (5)
3. The recent history of Germany and Japan shows that facism does not allow a country to develop over the long run. (10-11)
4. To ensure progress, we have to work for basic freedoms and democracy. (12)

Completed Outline

24. Political Activity

Rigoberta makes it clear that rather than others seeing poor people and poor people seeing themselves as helpless victims, poor people can be empowered and can empower themselves to demand social change.

T/F Questions (Paragraphs where the answer is found are indicated) 1. T (1); 2. F (2); 3. T (3); 4. T (4); 5. F (7)

Comprehension Questions Possible answers might be
1. Rigoberta was upset about linguistic barriers because she wanted to feel close to other Indian women, but they couldn't understand each other. (par. 2)

21

2. In Huehuetenango, Rigoberta realized that some Indian families were poorer than her own family. (3)

3. Rigoberta's ladino friend taught her Spanish, and also that there are some good ladinos. (4)

4. It was hard for Rigoberta to criticize a ladino because she didn't want to humiliate anyone, and she had always been treated as inferior by ladinos. (5)

Completed Outline

paragraphs

1: Organizing companeros
2: Overcoming barriers
3: An experience in Huehuetenango
4: A ladino friend
5-6: Changing attitude toward ladinos
7: Attitude of Rigoberta's ladino friend

Lightning Source UK Ltd.
Milton Keynes UK
UKHW021954130922
408787UK00005B/290

9 780521 657792